The Colors of Christmas

Six Sermons and
Object Lessons
for Advent
and Christmas

H. Michael Nehls

C.S.S. Publishing Co., Inc.
Lima, Ohio

THE COLORS OF CHRISTMAS

O86 2T

6862 / ISBN 0-89536-838-2

PRINTED IN U.S.A.

Table of Contents

Preface 5

Advent 1 — *Green, the Color of Life*
Children's Message 7
Sermon 9

Advent 2 — *Purple, the Color of Royalty*
Children's Message 13
Sermon 15

Advent 3 — *Red, the Color of Sacrifice*
Children's Message 19
Sermon 21

Advent 4 — *Blue, The Color of Eternity*
Children's Message 25
Sermon 27

**Christmas Eve/Day — *White, the Color of Purity
and Holiness***
Children's Message 31
Sermon 33

**Christmas 1 — *Gold, the Color of Wealth
and Riches***
Children's Message 37
Sermon 39

Preface

The Colors of Christmas is a program of worship services designed for the local congregation. It is for use during the Advent and Christmas seasons of the Church year. Both the children's message and the adult sermon follow the specific color theme for the day. Altar hangings and paraments should follow the color theme too, where this is possible.

Advent is a time of anticipation, a time of hope. As God's people in Christ, we look for the coming of Christ our Lord as the Babe of Bethlehem, as the Christ of Christmas. And, in a larger sense, we also look forward to Christ's coming again in glory.

In an attempt to better share the truths of this special season, I created the program, *The Colors of Christmas.* The idea first came to me on a Saturday morning, as I watched the women of our Altar Guild changing the paraments in the sanctuary. As the colors were changed, it came to me that Christmas is certainly a season of color. Why not, then, use the colors of the Advent/Christmas season to demonstrate the truths behind the great Gift of Christ in Christmas?

The entire program was developed in the summer of 1983 and used in St. Martin's Lutheran Church during Advent/Christmas of that same year. The children's message included a ribbon of the color theme for the day. Each child was given a different ribbon each Sunday and I wore one on my robe, too. The children certainly looked forward to the different color ribbons and enjoyed the program very much. Each week, we added a new ribbon until we wore all six. Many of the children wore all six ribbons several weeks after the program was completed.

The Colors of Christmas seeks to share the varied aspects of the birth, life, and glory of Jesus Christ, that God's people may prepare fully to celebrate His birth. To that end, I commend its use for others. May God alone be glorified.

H. Michael Nehls
September, 1985

Advent 1
Children's Message

Green!

Good morning, boys and girls. During the morning announcements today, I told you what the special color is for this morning. Do you remember what it is? That's right, *green*. Green is the color for the day. And what day is today? That's right, today is the first Sunday in Advent, the beginning of a new church year. Today also we begin to think about Christmas, that time when we all celebrate the birth of God's Son, Jesus. Each Sunday during this Advent/Christmas season, we will have a different color as our theme. This morning, we begin with the color green.

Can you name some things that are green in color? Grass and leaves? Those are good answers. Green is the color of life, of growth. Each Spring we look forward to the greening of the grass and the coming again of the leaves and plants. When God first created the world, what color do you think it was? Yes, I think it was probably green, too.

But green is also one of the primary Christmas colors. Can you think of some special "green" things of Christmas? The Christmas tree is a good answer. It is an evergreen tree. It is always green, isn't it? Is there anything else that's green for Christmas? The Advent wreath? Very good. There are a few other things some of the adults might remember. Holly and mistletoe are popular during the Christmas season. All of these things, especially the Christmas tree, the evergreen, remind us that God has given us life. And with the coming of Christmas, God is about to give us new life again, through the birth of his baby Son, Jesus.

So that you will remember that, I have in my brown bag this morning a green ribbon for each of you to wear. Each Sunday during this Christmas season, you will receive a different color ribbon. I want you to wear them, adding the new one each Sunday. Here is a green ribbon for each of you, and there is even one for me to wear on my robe. Now, what does the color of green remind us of? That's right, life and growth. God gives us life, in creation and in the birth of his Son, Jesus.

Genesis 1:1-5
John 1:1-5

Green, The Color of Life

These two sections of Scripture portray for us, in a panoramic way, the story of creation. Genesis teaches that in the beginning there was God who created all things. There was nothing in the beginning until God caused it to happen. He spoke, and creation became a reality. God created everything from nothing. And behold, it was very good!

In much the same way, John's Gospel also teaches us about creation. It begins just as the Genesis creation account: *in the beginning*. But John says more, proclaiming that God's own Son, the Word made flesh, Jesus, our Emmanuel was involved in this act of creation. "Without him was not anything made that was made!" Jesus, then, is the One through whom all things were created. We recognize the truth that life comes from him. He is the source of life, all life. The creating life has come through his own hand, by his powerful Word. Eternal life has come through his own death and resurrection. Through creation, Christ has given us the gift of life. Through his passion, death, and resurrection, he has given that gift of life eternal. So this holy child of Bethlehem, this babe in the Christmas manger, is also tbe creating, omni-present God. He, and he alone is the source of all life, both in this world and the next.

Green is the color of life. That fact most assuredly pervades our thinking when we consider the "Colors of Christmas"! In our Ohio outdoors today, there is a marked lack of the color green. The leaves are gone. Most plants have died from frost and exposure. We are in the season of late autumn, early winter. This is a time of dormancy in the life of most of Ohio's growing things. They hibernate, they go to sleep, they die.

Now, of course, there is a highly technical, scientific explanation as to what actually happens. My college biology suggests that the cholorophyll dies and the caroteen takes over, becoming pre-dominant. But we're not scientists. We simply know that in autumn and winter, the plants die and the leaves fall. That's all we know, and probably all we need to know about such a subject. We're just people trying to understand life . . . the gift of life given to us by Christ himself.

But, one of the important Colors of Christmas is green. We see that "green" and that "greenery" surrounding us at Christmas. Today, we see it here, in God's house, the church. We find it in our green paraments: on the altar, lectern, and pulpit, in the color of my stole and in my Cross, in the ribbons of life we gave the youngsters a few moments ago. And we also see green in the holly and mistletoe of the yuletide season. Our Advent wreath is green, and our Christmas tree and decorations in the sanctuary themselves will abound with green.

A good symbol of this created life we have in Christ — and of our Advent/Christmas season, too, may be found in this branch from a tree . . . an evergreen. We use "evergreen" as a name for a certain type of shrub or bush or tree. "Evergreen." But evergreen is also what it is. It is ever-green. We know that this type of tree is a symbol of life, for it never loses its needles or leaves in winter. Rather, this tree remains green — *ever* green — all year long. It is always filled with life, continually reminding us of the life — the gift of life here and eternally — that is ours in Jesus Christ.

Green is the color of life, but the color green can also have some negative connotations. When I mention the color "green" to you, what is the first thing that pops into your head? Do you think of Christmas trees, evergreens, the green leaves, plants, and grass of a summer day? Or do you think of something else that is green, something else that has replaced God in the minds of many, many people? I'm referring, of course, to the "idol" money! The love of money is referred to in the Bible as the root of all evil. Indeed, Paul told brother Timothy that very truth. And it can be true for us, too, if we let money become the "idol" of our lives, that which we worship above all else. But this green money has another side to it, too. Money can be a positive, powerful force in doing God's will, in helping others, if we will but use it properly. It's a fact: we cannot live in this world today without money. But we can do a lot of good with it. It's not meant to be hoarded, but invested for God's greater glory. We are but stewards of God's many and varied gifts.

During the announcements this morning, and in your Sunday bulletin, too, we heard and read about a local Christmas Cheer program. This program offers you and me a joyous way of sharing the blessings of God with others. Green money is needed and you can help. Likewise, on your Sunday envelope, there are many wonderful programs supported by our green dollars. Our own congregation depends upon our green money to continue to do the work we do. Money, when used properly, is an important tool, a life-giving tool for Christians, at Christmas time and all year long. But if it becomes our god, then, my friends, we're in real trouble. Then the love of money becomes the root of all evil. As responsible Christians, we need to make responsible decisions.

In the 23rd chapter of Luke's Gospel, Jesus spoke himself of the color green. Jesus referred to it as he was being led on his way to Golgotha, to be nailed to the wooden Cross and put to death. As he was going, the women of Jerusalem came weeping and wailing after Jesus. Jesus told the women that they should not weep for him, but for themselves and their children. For the days are coming, says the Lord, when Jerusalem itself will be destroyed. And it is then that we encounter these strangely prophetic words: "For if they do this when the wood is green, what will happen when it is dry?"

Jesus said that the wood was green in those latter days, but many believe today that the wood is very, very dry . . . that the end is near. And it is in this context that we gather today, to celebrate the beginning once more of Advent, looking for the Babe of Bethlehem and the Christ of glory who promises to come once more.

There is a beautiful relationship here, then, between the life we have on this earth, this place, and the hope of eternal life that is ours in Christ. We know that both "lives" are gifts from our Lord. And this color green reminds us of life . . . the life God has given us . . . the life we live in his love and forgiveness.

I pray that this holiday season might be for each of us a season of life, a season of green. May we find in our preparation, our anticipation, and our celebration that intangible something from God that makes this life — all life — really worth the living! Have a blessed, green, life-filled holiday season, in Jesus Christ, our Lord.

Advent 2
Children's Message

Violet or Purple!

Good morning, boys and girls. I'm happy to see so many of you wearing your green ribbons this morning. See, I have mine, too. What does the color "green" remind us of? That's right, life and growth. Very good. Yes, God has given us all things in creation, including his Son, Jesus. Green reminds us of the life we have in his love, and is certainly a good color for the Christmas season. Just look at the beautiful green Christmas tree today!

We have a new color this morning, another color of Christmas. What color did I mention during my announcements? That's right. Purple or violet. And here, I have a purple ribbon for each of you to wear. This morning, a few of the women from our Senior Choir are going to help you pin your ribbons on while I tell you about purple or violet.

Now why is purple a good color for Christmas? Any ideas? This may be a bit more difficult to understand for us, since purple isn't that common for the Christmas season, is it? Purple is the color of royalty. Kings and princes often wear purple robes as a symbol of their authority and power. And who is the great King of kings, whose birthday we're preparing to celebrate? That's right, Jesus. So, because Jesus is our great King, purple is a wonderful color for Christmas.

Do you see anything that is violet or purple in the sanctuary this morning? That's right, the altar cloths or paraments. Anything else? Very good, the candles on the Advent wreath. They are purple . . . the candles for the King. Anything else? Well, there is one more place, but you can't see it from here. Purple is also the color of grapes, and what do many people make out of grapes? Wine? Yes, wine. This morning, we will celebrate Holy Communion, the coming of the King, Jesus to each of us in a special way. And we celebrate this Lord's Supper with bread and wine, prepared and waiting for us on the altar.

Purple, violet. It reminds us of what? That's right, that Jesus is the King of kings. Other kings came seeking Jesus, too. We call them the Wise Men. All in all, purple is a great color of Christmas!

Luke 1:31-35
                                          Luke 23:33-38

Violet, The Color of Royalty

"Prepare the royal highway . . . the King of Kings is near!" This is Advent! Together, as God's people in Jesus Christ, we look for the coming of our Lord. Last Sunday morning, we began our celebration of the Advent/Christmas season with a look at the "Colors of Christmas!" For our first color, our emphasis last Sunday was on green — the color of life. We spoke of Christ Jesus, the Babe of Bethlehem as the source of all life, both life in this world and life for all believers in the next. Today, we look at violet or purple — the color of royalty. It is the color of kings, and especially the King of kings whose birth is certainly drawing near!

As a prelude to our consideration this morning, I'd like to share with you two portions of God's Word, from the Gospel of Luke. First, Luke 1:31-35 and then Luke 23:33-38.

From the beginning of Luke's Gospel, until the very end of it, we find Jesus, our Lord, called King. The angel announced it at his conception and birth. The Jews, on the other hand, sarcastically proclaimed Jesus as King of the Jews as he died on the Cross for the sins of all the world. Jesus the King . . . the royal Son of David. In birth and in death, he is called King. "Prepare the royal highway . . . the King of kings is near!"

A royal King, standing in the line of David, was exactly what the Jews were looking for when Jesus was born. The society of Israel to which Jesus came was a society filled with oppression. Rome was in absolute control. They exacted tribute from their Jewish subjects. No one dared oppose their rule. A few had tried, and most of them had paid the ultimate price. And so, the Jews longed for a new prince, a new King, a new Anointed One, a Messiah like David to restore Judah to its lofty place of political prominence.

History is very important to the Jewish people. Following the death of David and Solomon, and with the assumption of the throne by King Rehoboam, the nation of Israel had suffered from internal strife and continual decline. No King was remembered more fondly than King David. So, remember him they did. For it was David who had consolidated the territory of Israel and expanded the nation. It was David who had established Jerusalem as Israel's capital. It was David who had won many great victories over Israel's enemies. And it was David who had founded a dynasty of kings. And so it was David who was remembered reverently, hopefully. Wouldn't it be great if we could just have another king like David? If only King David would return and throw the Romans out! The prophets fueled this longing for another David through the continual promises of God.

For example, in our first lesson for this morning, Isaiah calls for a shoot, a branch from the stump of Jesse. You remember Jesse, David's father. Likewise, our Psalm for the day is a Psalm of Solomon. It is actually a prayer of blessing for a righteous king.

Though their powerful nation was gone . . . though kings like David no longer existed, still the Jews remembered . . . they remembered King David and longed for such royalty once more.

It was into this world of remembering and anticipation that Jesus came. Tha angel called him King. The Wise Men recognized him in the same way: "Where is he who has been born King of the Jews?" But in reality, Jesus was just the opposite of the great king and military leader the people were hoping for. The Jews expected power, authority, military victories and revolt. Instead, Jesus came filled with (in the words of Isaiah this morning) "the spirit of wisdom and understanding, the spirit of council and justice, the spirit of knowledge and the fear of the Lord!"

And it was Isaiah's prophecy that came true in the life and teachings of Jesus of Nazareth. He fulfilled all that was spoken about him concerning the prophets. But the Jews . . . ah, well, the Jews! They just didn't know what to make of this Jesus. They missed the royal King when he came knocking on their door. Only at Jesus' death, did they call him King . . . King of the Jews, but this was simply a cruel, humorless joke.

In retrospect, how can we blame them? Given their political situation and their longings for a king, how can we blame them? Did Jesus look like a king? Did he act like a king? How was this Jesus dressed? Did he wear the purple robe of a king?

Actually, he *did* wear a purple robe once in his life. Mark's Gospel reports that as Jesus was taken as a prisoner to the palace, the soldiers clothed Jesus in a purple cloak and plaiting a crown of thorns, they put it on him. And they began to salute him, "Hail, King of the Jews!" And they struck him with a reed and spit upon him, and they knelt down in mock homage to him. And when they mocked him they stripped him of the purple cloak, and put his own clothes on him, and they led him out to be crucified.

Purple, violet is the color of royalty. It is reserved for kings' palaces, not mangers and stables. Yet purple, violet is a color of Christmas. It is the color we generally see hanging from the altar, lectern, pulpit, and pastor during Advent. It is the color we use during the Lenten season, too, since it is also a color of repentance.

The color violet; the King; and repentance have a lot in common. Our sins have been confessed this morning. And we know that because of Christ, our King, because of his loving death for our sake, our sins have been eliminated, washed away. This King, our King, our royal King Jesus sacrificed himself for his subjects. He took off the purple robe in heaven, and put on the diapers of Bethlehem for our sake. He took off the purple robe in Herod's palace, willingly laying down his life on the Cross for our sake.

The color for today, this color of Christmas, is violet . . . and we use it, we wear it, so that we may never, ever forget what he has done for us all.

In another way, remembering will be part of our worship this morning, too. On the evening before Jesus died, He took a cup of wine . . . wine made from purple grapes, just like these, and mysteriously, miraculously changed the eating habits of Christians forever. For as we gather here, Advent comes true . . . the King comes to us once more, through his own Body, his own Blood. We celebrate, we rejoice, we remember, we repent!

"Prepare the royal highway . . . the King of kings is near!" Violet is the color of royalty! As you gather during this holiday season with family and friends, may you remember whose birthday we are celebrating. May you remember the angel's message. "For to you is born this day in the city of David, a Savior, a Messiah, who is Christ the Lord!" That Babe born in Bethlehem, so very long ago is Christ the King . . . your king . . . my king!

Violet — the color of royalty. "Then greet the King of glory . . . foretold in sacred story. Hosanna to the Lord . . . for He fulfills God's Word!"

Advent 3
Children's Message

Red!

Good morning, boys and girls. I'm pleased to see each of you wearing your ribbons this morning. Let's go over them together. The green ribbon reminds us of life and growth, doesn't it? And the purple one? That's correct, that Jesus is the King of kings! Very good. Notice that I'm wearing my green and purple ribbons this morning, too!

Well, this morning's color certainly fits the Christmas season, doesn't it? What color is it? That's right, it's Red. Red is probably the best known color of the Christmas season. Can you name me some things that are red that we often associate with Christmas? Santa Claus. Yes that's a good answer. Santa's suit is bright red, isn't it. Rudolf's nose? That's another good answer. Many of the Christmas presents under the Christmas tree are red, too, aren't they? Red ribbons and bows, red wrapping paper, candy canes . . . those are all good answers.

Well, this morning I want to tell you about a few more items that make red such an excellent color for Christmas. Here are your red ribbons and one for me, too. Let's ask the women of the senior choir to help you again as I talk about red as a color of Christmas.

Red is the color of blood, of sacrifice. If you would cut your finger, even just a little bit, what would come out of the cut? That's right, blood. And what color is blood? Yes, it's red . . . bright red. Christmas is the celebration of the birth of God's Son, Jesus. And Jesus came to this earth to live, and to die. Jesus died on the Cross to save us from our sins. He sacrificed himself, gave his blood, that we might belong to God forever. So with red, we remember to celebrate Christmas, and what it means for God to love us enough that he would sacrifice, give up his own Son. So red is a good color of Christmas. It means a lot more than just Santa Claus, presents, and candy canes, though, doesn't it? It reminds us that Jesus died on the Cross to save us all!

Advent 3
Genesis 22:1-14
Matthew 2:16-18

Red, the Color of Sacrifice

Of all the colors of Christmas, I suppose red is the most prominent. Look around you, in our beautiful sanctuary this morning. We see red bows, red lights, red paper . . . even the paraments, the cross around my neck, and the ribbons I gave the youngsters today are red. But there is more of a meaning to the "red" of Christmas than all of these red things that surround us today.

Just as the green spoke to us of life two weeks ago, and violet or purple suggested the royalty of Christ last Sunday, today red has a special meaning, too. I alluded to it with the youngsters, but I want to take it one step further with all of you. God's Word sheds some light on this meaning of sacrifice, and I'd like to look at fourteen verses of the 22nd chapter of Genesis, followed by just two verses, verses 16-18 of Matthew's second chapter. *Read the text!*

In the Genesis story I just read, we see old Abraham, now well past one hundred years of age, willing to sacrifice his young, probably teen-age son, just because the Lord God told him it was the thing to do.

Isaac meant a lot to his father Abraham. And no wonder. Abraham and Sarah had tried for years and years to have a son. But Sarah just never became pregnant. There were no great medical specialists in those days, so Abraham and Sarah had contented themselves with the knowledge that for some reason, they would not have a son, an heir.

But then God entered the picture. He made a promise,

an agreement, a covenant with Abraham. He told Abraham that he would be the father of a great nation. That the descendants of their family would be as the sands of the sea. Sarah laughed when she heard about God's promise. But even at age ninety, God could still work a miracle in this laughing wife of Abraham. And he did. Isaac was born and they believed the promise of God. There was more than just a great nation connected to the promise. God had said that, through their descendants, one would come to set right all that had gone wrong. A Messiah, a Savior was the promise.

But now all of that was in jeopardy as Isaac and Abraham climbed the mountain. Sacrifice his own son, tie him to the altar and kill him with a knife? That had been the command of God and Abraham sought to obey. It looked as if the promise would be lost in the red blood of Isaac, slain as a sacrifice to God. First the altar, then the wood, then the ropes, then the knife. And suddenly, as the knife was drawn forth, the hand of God intervened. It had been a test, a test of faith. And so the son, the heir, was saved. The blood was not shed.

This is a remarkable story, filled with so much of Christmas. God willingly sent his own son to earth, laid him in the manger at Bethlehem. God the Father knew that it meant real sacrifice, that indeed, the red blood of Jesus must be shed for the sins of the world. Like Abraham, God did not withhold his son of promise, but willingly gave him up for the sins of mankind.

In the second reading, we find that this baby Jesus has been spared. The Wise Men had been warned not to return to Herod, so they didn't. Instead, they departed for their homeland by another way. Herod, realizing that he had been tricked by the Wise Men, decided to do away with Jesus himself. He sent his soldiers to Bethlehem, and the slaughter was underway. Herod sacrificied the blood of hundreds of youngsters for his own selfish gain. Again, just as at the Cross, red blood was shed and weeping was heard!

Both stories deal with sacrifice, and give us a prelude to the events of Good Friday. I guess that whether we like to think about it or not, Jesus was born into this world to die. He came to Bethlehem as a baby, but the road would lead to Calvary and his own death. "Come thou long expected Jesus, born to set thy people free!"

It's interesting to note that in reality we know precious little about the birth of Christ. John and Mark mention it not at all. Matthew has a scant seven verses dealing with Jesus' birth. The rest we learn from St. Luke and that is only some twenty verses. No, the birth of Jesus has its importance only as a prelude to the death and resurrection of our Lord. It is in looking back at Jesus' sacrifice for the sins of the world, that his birth, his incarnation take on majestic meaning!

But lest we spend all of our time with long faces this third Sunday in Advent, let us remember that red is also the color of celebration and rejoicing. Red shines about us at Christmas . . . in packages shared, in candy canes consumed, in Santa's red suit, in the glow of children's faces! Red is the color of celebration and joy. The same is true in the Church. We use red for our festival holidays: Reformation, Confirmation, Ordination. And we also use red to celebrate the Church's birthday, the festival of Pentecost! So, red is truly a color of Christmas, fitting both in the home and in the church. For just as we use it to celebrate the Church's birthday, we should use it to celebrate Christ's birthday. The two are inseparably linked together.

Christmas Day is two weeks from today. Red poinsettia will adorn the sanctuary. We will celebrate the birth of Jesus. But as we celebrate, as we worship, as we gather with our families around the altar and the colorful Christmas tree, let us remember that our Lord Jesus came joyously, courageously at Christmas, came as the perfect Lamb of God, the sacrifice for all of our sins.

Sacrifice is a tough word for us. It's difficult to understand. We have so much in life . . . and we are asked to give so little. But God gave everything he had, the greatest Christmas gift ever, that the red blood of Jesus Christ might cleanse us forever, bringing us back into the perfect relationship with him.

One good way for us to remember this red sacrifice might be through the love God has given us. The heart, like the heart of a giant red Valentine, is the center of such love. And God gives his very heart to us at Christmas. May its red glow, and may all the red of Christmas, remind us of that love, that celebration, that sacrifice for us . . . in the name of Christ, our Lord!

Advent 4
Children's Message

Blue!

Good morning, boys and girls. What color ribbons do we have this morning? Blue. Yes, we have blue ribbons today. Blue is our color of Christmas for this morning. But, before we pass out the blue ribbons and talk about them, let's review the first three we already have. First, we have green. The green ribbon stands for what? Correct, life and growth. Next, we have the purple ribbon. It reminds us that Jesus is the King of kings. And last Sunday's ribbon was red. Through the color red, we remember that Jesus died on the Cross to save us all.

And now the blue ribbons. Once again, the women of the senior choir will help you pin on your blue ribbons while I talk to you about the color blue as a color of Christmas.

This morning, the altar paraments are blue in color, just like our ribbons. Blue. When a new baby is born, and the baby happens to be a little girl, in what color is she often dressed? Pink, that's correct. And, what color is used if the baby is a boy? That's right, blue. Blue seems to be the color for boys, doesn't it? But there's more behind the color blue than the fact that Jesus was a baby boy. Blue is also the color of heaven or eternity. What color is the sky on a bright and sunny day like today? That's correct, it's blue. Likewise, when we think of water, what color comes to mind? Blue again. And what do we use water for in the Church? Baptism, that's right. When most of you were little babies, you were brought here to the altar and baptized. The pastor took water and poured it over your head, so that you might become a child of God. During the Christmas season, we remember once more the coming of the Child of God, Jesus. He came down to us from heaven. He was baptized by John the Baptizer in the Jordan River. His is God's Son and our Savior for eternity.

As you can see, there are several good reasons that blue is one of the colors of Christmas. Wear your blue ribbon proudly. It reminds us of the baby boy, born in Bethlehem, Jesus, our eternal Savior! And through the color blue, we can remember our baptism also as a Child of God!

Blue, The Color of Eternity

I once heard of a dream about Christmas. It's not the usual dream of a baby boy in the manger in the stable at Bethlehem. Rather, the dream goes something like this:

One day, our Lord Jesus entered the office of the angel in charge of foreign relations in heaven. "I just heard that I might be making a trip down to earth. . ." The angel allowed his gold pencil two taps on his desk. "That's right . . . and soon, too." "Well," continues Jesus, "what I want to know is where? Where on earth? Rome? Athens? Corinth? Alexandria? There's a fine library in Alexandria, and I hear that the Emperor's symphony at Rome is even better than the Athens Philharmonic, and I would love to see the Parthenon in person, too. . ." His voice trailed off.

Without speaking, the angel got up, went over to the large map on the wall. He took his pencil and found the Mediterranean Sea; he touched Rome. Jesus' heart stopped for a moment . . . then moved east to Corinth and Athens . . . the Lord held his breath. The pencil continued to move east, then south. The angel seemed to be having a little trouble finding the place he was looking for. Then he spotted Jerusalem; holding the pencil point on Jerusalem, he looked around it in a small circle. "I guess it's just too little to be on the map." "Too little? What's too little?" the Lord asked. "Bethlehem" was the answer.

"Bethlehem!" The Lord's jaw dropped. "You mean I'm going to Bethlehem?" The angel didn't deny it. "But . . . but there's nothing there, nothing at all. No symphonies, no libraries, no works of art, no centers of learning. There won't even be decent living accommodations . . . just a little run-down inn! How can I set up my office there?"

The angel cleared his throat and tried to find just the right words. "We weren't thinking of having you set up an office . . . you'll be going steerage this trip."

"Steerage! No office . . . Bethlehem! I had hoped for something a little better than Bethlehem. Well, I might as well start packing."

At this point, the angel put his hand on the Lord's shoulder. "Umm, that won't be necessary! I don't know how to tell you this, but we're sending you in the same way all humans enter the world . . . we're sending you as a baby."

There was a long, long silence. "As a baby! As a *baby*? Are you sure . . . why, there isn't even a decent hospital in Bethlehem!"

"I know . . . I know," said the angel gently. "You'll just have to make the best of things."

Slowly the Lord walked out of the angel's office, mumbling to himself, "To Bethlehem . . . not to Rome, or Corinth, or Athens. Bethlehem? To a little dingy, dirty, out of-the-way place like Bethlehem . . . and going as a baby on top of it all! Bethlehem, of all places! With my luck, the inn will probably be full up when I arrive!"

At Christmas, Jesus came to earth as a baby boy! The mighty Son of God . . . the Lord of all nations . . . the Prince of Peace! A baby . . . a little baby boy. As we know that the color blue is the color of baby boys!

But, like the green, the violet, and the red that have preceeded it, blue has a deeper meaning as well. It is also the color of eternity. It reminds us of heaven, of the place where we are going in order to be with God, the place from where Jesus came in the first place! Eternity . . . a relationship we have with this little baby boy of Bethlehem. It's a relationship that is borne out, that begins, with baptism. Listen with me to the words of St. Paul from Romans, the sixth chapter. [Read the text]

Alive to God in Jesus Christ! Doesn't sound much like the Christmas story, does it? More like Easter? Exactly! And that's the point. This baby boy, dressed in blue as a color of Christmas, is the same victorious Christ of Easter. And the victory, the glory, the hope and promise of eternity is ours, through the blue water of baptism!

My little "dream" about Jesus descending to earth as a child, I believe, points out vividly to what great lengths God our Father went to save us, his children. His only begotten Son, reduced to a mere infant, a baby boy, the child of Bethlehem.

In our Gospel lesson for this morning, Matthew tells the story of the angel's appearance to Joseph. What a conversation Joseph and Mary must have had the night before! "You're what? Pregnant? What a disgrace! You're nothing but a harlot! You've ruined my reputation and your own!"

But the angel comes with these words: "Joseph, do not fear to take Mary your wife, for that which is conceived in her is of the Holy Spirit; she will bear a son, and you shall call his name Jesus, for he will save his people from their sins!" So the gift God gave the world at Christmas was the greatest gift he could possibly give. His own Son, his own little boy, the Child who comes to give us the gift of eternity!

Reading through a December issue of Readers Digest this past week, I came across this little story that shares with us much of the truth of Christmas:

"There once was an African boy who gave his missionary teacher an exquisite sea shell as a Christmas gift. The lad had walked miles and miles for it, to a special bay, the only place where such sea shells were found. "How wonderful of you to have traveled so far for this present," said the teacher. The boy's eyes shone as he replied, "Long walk, part of gift!"

It was a long walk from Nazareth to Bethlehem, from eternity to Bethlehem, but the long walk was part of God's gift . . . that we might know eternity . . . that we might experience life as God intended . . . that we might be with him forever!

"Blue . . . the color of eternity. One of the Colors of Christmas. Think about your baptism, God's gift to you of the baby boy at Bethlehem, as you celebrate your Christmas in a few short days. Because of the Christ of Christmas, we have the gift of eternity. Enjoy your gift, your Christmas gift from God this Christmas. Joy to the world, the Lord has come!

Christmas Eve or Day
Children's Message

White!

Good evening, boys and girls. Merry Christmas to each of you. Tonight, I have another ribbon for each of you. It's a special ribbon tonight, and a special color, the color *white*. It's good to see many of you wearing your four colored ribbons this evening. I have my four ribbons, too. Together, let's review the colors. The green one stands for life and growth. That's what Jesus gives each of us. The purple one reminds us that Jesus is — what? The King of kings, that's right. And the red one? It helps us remember that Jesus died on the Cross to save us from our sins. And last Sunday, I gave you your blue ribbon. The blue one reminds us of many things. We think of heaven, the blue sky, the baby boy, Jesus, and also our baptism. Well, each of these ribbons has been but a prelude to the ribbons I'm giving you this evening. Let's ask the women of the senior choir to help you pin them on, as I share with you once more the story of Christmas.

Tonight and tomorrow, we celebrate the birth of Jesus. How many of you remember when you were born? We can't remember back that far, can we? But how many of you have younger brothers or sisters? Okay. Do you recall how excited everyone was when they were born? Your parents were just as happy, just as thrilled when you were born! And you can imagine then, all the joy in earth and heaven when Jesus was born! The angels came from heaven to sing at Jesus' birth. The shepherds left their sheep to come and see this special Child of God. Mary wrapped Jesus in some cloths and probably put something that looks like this on Jesus. What is it? That's right, a diaper. So do you see why white as the perfect color for Christmas. Angels, sheep, diapers. But there's even more. White is the color of purity and holiness. It represents Jesus as the spotless Lamb of God. White also reminds us of the fluffy white snow that blankets the ground for almost every Christmas. It's as though God's purifying the whole earth through the coming of his holy Son, Jesus.

I'm sure you're excited about Christmas. I am, too. We all are. But during all of the excitement, let's remember the purity, the holiness, the color of this season . . . white. Jesus is the perfect Son of God. Let's celebrate his birthday together, singing his praises, just like the angels. We have one more color of Christmas, and I'll share that with you this Sunday. I'll see you then. Have a Merry Christmas!

Christmas Day   Luke 2:1-20

White, The color of purity, holiness

Yesteday morning, amid the cold, the snow, and the blowing wind, I ventured down to the church to work on this Christmas message. I made two stops on the way . . . one at the gas station to top off my gas tank. There I saw several cars being jumped, pushed, coaxed, and begged into running. I was very thankful that my key brought the engine to life. My other stop was at the grocery store to pick up a gallon of milk. The store was busy, crowded with people picking up those last minute necessities for Christmas, and of course, just in case the weather worsened and we were all snowed in.

As I stood in line at the check-out, an older gentleman was talking to a friend. They were discussing the terrible weather, and the one man remarked that this certainly had to be the worst Christmas weather he could remember. Well, such a remark, directed at the older gentleman, was bound to ellicit the remark. "Well, I can remember a Christmas with weather even worse than this. When I was a boy, we had a Christmas even worse than this. When I was a boy, we had a Christmas of weather eighteen below, and six feet of snow. The wind was blowing and drifting the snow." He went on to describe a bitter cold day, but one on which much warmth and love was shared among family and friends.

This conversation prompted several thoughts in my mind as I considered this Christmas festival. First of all, though the weather outside is frightful, inside, with all of you it's so delightful! Today, with our modern ways of heating our homes, our cars, our churches, we can live in relative comfort in spite of the weather. We have learned how to conquer, if not control, the environment. So this Christmas, though perhaps one of the coldest ever, can be one of the warmest because of the conveniences of our modern world. We are warm and comfortable in here, [and those who could not get to church this morning need only listen to their radio and we will bring the Christmas Day service of St Martin's Lutheran Church right Into their homes.]* The "good old days" have a lot of fond memories for many, but on a day like today I'm thankful for our technological achievements. Thank-you, good Lord!

Second, we've often heard the phrase, "Christmas is for kids!" In many ways that does seem true enough. Most of our best memories of Christmas are of those special Christmases when we were children. The beautiful gifts, the magnificent Christmas tree, those great "goodies" to eat, and that part we all had to memorize for the Sunday church school Christmas program are the things that pop into our heads when we think of Christmas. Those special times live again, anew each year as we decorate, wrap, and prepare ourselves for the holiday season. And the Christmas of today will be for some of us, especially the youngsters, the glorious memory of Christmas tomorrow. Someday, when they are as old and wise as we adults, they will remark, "Why I remember a Christmas when it was bitter cold; few were able to get out, to come and worship; yet it was perhaps the best Christmas ever!

Finally, the third idea that popped into my mind is this: where must we all be today? It's in Bethlehem, on another cold winter day, when Mary, God's chosen woman, gave birth to her first-born son, wrapped him in swaddling cloths and laid him in a manger. Listen again, with me, to that old, old story of the greatest Christmas ever, Luke

---

*Adapt for local use.

2:1-20. *[Read the text]*

Christmas is Jesus' birthday. On Christmas, God touched the earth with his love, his forgiveness, his peace, his purity and holiness for all people. The color white is certainly that color. White snow, the white glow of candlelight on a child's face, the whiteness of angel's wings as they share good news of a great joy, the whiteness of the Lamb of God who comes to take away the sin of the world, the whiteness of a newborn baby's diaper. Purity and holiness in Christ our Lord.

Perhaps the man was right. Christmas *is* for kids, for it was as a child that Jesus came and he tells us that we must come with child-like faith to understand his love and receive his blessing. And don't we all become children again at Christmas? Aren't we innocent and pure once more, looking forward and yet looking back to Christmases long ago — and to the first Christmas long, long ago? In the spirit of God's love and the truth of Christmas, I'd like to close with the words of a simple Christmas poem, a special poem for this special day:

In that little stable so long ago
  There were no dazzling lights.
There was nothing to distract one's thoughts
  From that precious, holy sight.

High above the brilliant star
  Was shining down from heaven.
And in the stillness of that moment
  God's wondrous gift was given.

Shepherds came from near and far
  Their hearts were filled with love
And watching o'er the little child
  Were angels from above.

The three Wise Men bearing gifts
   At last on him did gaze.
And as they looked in wonderment
   Their lips were uttering praise.

So take a moment to recall
   How this season did begin,
And make your heart a quiet stable
   Where the Lord may enter in.

May the peace, joy, the holiness and purity that is Christmas be yours, giving you comfort, confidence, for the new year! Merry Christmas, my friends!

Amen.

First Sunday after Christmas
Children's Message

Gold!

Good morning, boys and girls. It's good to see all of you here. Did you have a Merry Christmas? That's great! Wow! Look at all of those ribbons you're wearing this morning. How many do you have? That's right! We each have five ribbons. A green one that stands for life; a purple one that stands for Jesus, the King of kings; a red one that reminds us of the sacrifice Jesus has made for us; a blue one that teaches us that Jesus, God's Son, came down from heaven; and a white one that represents the perfect Son of God, Jesus our Savior.

Today, you will receive your last ribbon from me. What color is it? Gold. Aren't these gold ribbons pretty? They look great with the others. Gold is the color of wealth and riches. When someone has something gold colored, we think of it as being expensive, worth a great deal of money. Gold was one of the gifts brought to Jesus by . . . whom? The Wise Men, that's correct. The Wise Men brought great treasures to Jesus, gifts of gold, frankincense, and myrrh. Gold also represents the Star of Bethlehem that guided the Wise Men as they searched for Jesus. Finally, the straw of the manger is gold in color. Though Jesus is the greatest king ever, his birth was lowly and humble, born in a stable behind the Bethlehem inn.

The Colors of Christmas — you have them represented by ribbons, green, purple, red, blue, white, and gold. I hope you'll keep your ribbons, that each Christmas they may remind you of all we've learned about Christ Jesus and Christmas this year. Thanks for sharing in this special time with me as we've talked about the Colors of Christmas together. Let's celebrate the truth of Christmas each day throughout this coming year. God bless you all!

Gold, The Color of Wealth and Riches

As we face a new year, it is customary in America to greet one another with the phrase, "Happy New Year!"

But, New Year's Day may not be that happy for some. On New Year's morning, many, many people across our land are not happy with their headaches and hangovers because of the previous evening's excessive dining, drinking, and dancing. And how can we be happy if the new year is just more of the same old things . . . the same poverty, unemployment, inflation, nuclear arms race, sickness, war, and failure? When we reflect upon things even just briefly, we certainly have cause to ask the question, "Just what's so great, what's "happy" about the new year?"

Now, lest we bury our heads in our hands and give up, even before the new year has begun, let's consider what happened one week ago this morning. You know, Christmas! You remember Christmas, don't you? It was in all the papers. It's the biggest holiday of the year. There's a Christmas tree, lots of presents, Santa Claus comes, it falls on December 25th. Ah, yes, you remember about Christmas, don't you?

But there is more, much more to Christmas than all that stuff. And that's what makes the new year happy. "For to you is born in the city of David a Savior who is Christ the Lord!" God has come to show us how to live, how to live together in joy, hope, and peace for all people. He came at Christmas to make a difference in people's lives — in your life and mine.

One thing is sure: the coming of Jesus as the Babe of Bethlehem certainly made the difference in the lives of those Wise Men from the East. They traveled many, many miles just to offer gifts to the newborn King of the Jews. Let's have a look and a listen to their story as Matthew tells it in Matthew 2:1-12. *[Read the text]*

And they offered him gifts, gold and frankincense and myrrh. When we think of gold, we think of riches, wealth, and power. And it is certainly that. In our world, in this society, the person with gold — with money — has wealth, riches, and power. But gold is also a color. Consider the beautiful gold ribbons I gave the youngsters this morning. Gold is bright, the color of sunlight and starlight, the color of straw, all of these reminding us of our Lord's most humble birth.

And isn't the coming of the Christ of Christmas the real wealth of the season, the riches of a new year that is just beginning? It is the love of God, Jesus Christ, our Lord!

Those Wise Men were rich. They came bringing with them gifts, treasures fit for a king. The gifts represented much wealth. Yet, when the Magi saw this little baby, poor and humble, in the arms of his mother, a simple young maiden, they fell down and worshiped him. They recognized that in this child, the earth had been blessed in a special way by God. So they humbled themselves, offered their great treasures, knelt and gave homage to Jesus.

And when this same Jesus grew up, he taught people about riches and how they are to be used. "Do not lay up for yourselves treasures on earth, where moth and rust consume and where thieves break in and steal, but lay up for yourselves treasures in heaven, where neither moth nor rust consumes and where thieves do not break in and steal. For where your treasure is, there will your heart be also."

Here our Lord is not speaking of saving money. He's

speaking instead of saving souls. Money, riches, wealth, power, gold is not to become our idol, our god that we put above God. We must be willing to give it up. We are to be Christians, believers in Christ and his love first and foremost.

Some time ago, a man handed me a card with the question on it, "If you were arrested for being a Christian, would there be enough evidence to convict you?" That makes me stop and think. Are we Christians in our day-to-day living? Are we putting our treasures in heaven? Are we taking a stand against evil and for the right, or are we compromising so well with the world that it is impossible to tell a Christian from a non-Christian?

We can become too "relevant to the world" so that we forget who we are. We loose our distinctiveness as Christians. There was once a man who loved the color yellow. He had yellow carpet in his home. He also had yellow drapes, yellow furniture, a yellow bedspread, and yellow pajamas. But, one day he became very sick. He contracted yellow jaundice. His wife sent for the doctor who went right to his home to examine him. His wife showed the doctor into the man's bedroom. Shortly, the doctor came out of the room. The wife asked immediately how her husband was doing. The physician replied, "How's he doing? I don't know. I couldn't find him!"

We, likewise, must be careful, watchful, that we do not become lost in the worldly ways of our age. Like the Wise Men of old, we must learn to give our gifts, our gold, away if it is to accomplish the purpose for which God intended. Gifts are, after all, only gifts *when they are given to someone else.*

Our last color of the Christmas season is gold. As we face the new year, may we learn the golden lesson the Wise Men shared, that to be happy and at peace in this world, we must place our God first, above all things, all gifts, all gold. It is in doing this that we will understand what wealth is.

As you begin the new year, as you join with me here at our Lord's Table, may you receive the most precious gift God offers you this holiday season . . . himself. May you find a wealth of happiness and joy in his great love for you. Have a happy, blessed, peaceful, and joyful new year. My friends, Happy New Year!

About the Author

H. Michael Nehls is pastor of St. Martin's Lutheran Church in Archbold, Ohio, where he has served for the past six years. He is a graduate of Capital University and Trinity Lutheran Seminary, the latter with honors. Pastor Nehls is active in conference and district work of The American Lutheran Church, having completed a term as the Michigan District Secretary and member of the Executive Committee.

A native of Oak Harbor, Ohio, Pastor Nehls and his wife, Ivy are the parents of two daughters, Stefanie, fourteen, and Melanie, ten. They are active campers and Pastor Nehls enjoys an occasional round of golf. Other hobbies include restoration of antique automobiles and collecting Civil War memorabilia.

Pastor Nehls has also done post-graduate work at Oregon State University and Trinity Lutheran Seminary. This, his first publication, examples what he enjoys doing most of all: preaching God's Word.